Signatures

Enslaved

A Chronicle of Resistance
Book 1 – The Lamentation of the Enslaved

By
Brian Sankarsingh

And featuring poems by
Janet L. Wheat-Kaytor
J. E. Rehel
Loretta Laurie Fisher
Sherman K. Francis

SG Productions

First Edition 2023

All rights reserved.

No part of this publication may be reproduced in any form, or by any means, electronic or mechanical, including photocopying, recording, or any information browsing, storage, or retrieval system without permission in writing from SG Productions except in the case of brief quotations embodied in critical reviews and certain other non-commercial uses permitted by copyright law.

For permission requests, write to:
Sankarsingh Gonsalves Productions
c\o brian@sgproductions.ca

ISBN
Softcover 978-1-7777968-7-7
Hardcover 978-1-7777968-8-4

Poetry, Canadian

Praise for Enslaved, A Chronicle of Resistance

"Enslaved" is a very worthy book series! Especially for educational institutions. I am indeed happy to endorse and promote "the Enslaved series" at A Different Booklist bookstore! – **Itah Sadu, award-winning storyteller and author, managing director of the Blackhurst Cultural Centre and co-owner of A Different Booklist.**

***

Overall, the book (Enslaved, A Chronicle of Resistance Lamentation of the Enslaved) with a focus on the beginning period of enslavement is a very good educational tool or resource mainly for young adults and youth. It introduces them to the facts of the Atlantic Slave Trade. Young people might not necessarily want to read a textbook account about African enslavement. Poetry can be more digestible at times, and it is an alternative way to expose them to that history and to important related themes. For example, that there was much resistance on the part of the enslaved; and they did not just passively accept the brutality imposed on them. I also appreciated the poems: "Stripped" and "I am Human" because they made very clear that the only way for the enslavement of Africans to happen on such a monstrous scale was by the belief that Africans were not fully human. It is an important point to make because it introduced a conversation about the immorality of the entire practice. People need to know not only the facts and details of what happened, but why it happened and also why it should never happen again." **Geeta Raghunanan, A Different Booklist**

***

First and foremost, I feel privileged to have been asked to review this amazing work by a good friend and colleague. I don't consider myself a literary person nor I consider myself a person engaged with history as such. I like to read, and I attempt to familiarize myself with history with the aim of understanding the present.

I am honored to lead an organization established to address the impact of anti-Black racism on the health and wellbeing of Black communities. Reading the series 'Enslaved, A Chronicle of Resistance', not only re-affirmed for me the importance of the movement that uplifts the voice, the struggle, the strength and the dreams and aspirations of the diverse Black communities which was intensified after the painful deaths of George Floyd, Brianna Taylor, Regis Korchinski-Paquet, Joyce Echaquan and many more; but also reminded me that addressing systemic anti-Black racism is a very long and complex journey because it is hidden in plain sight!

Not all good will gestures by the system players are meant to bring about positive change and wellbeing for Black communities. In one of the poems, John Brown, the captain of the ship, has kept the vessel well ventilated. Plainly this is a noble gesture to keep his 'cargo' healthy. But hidden is the motive of preserving the value of the 'cargo' so there is no financial loss. How are we to receive certain legislations, policies, promises from the ship owners and captains of today? Do they have our true wellbeing in mind or does it continue to be about their own self-preservation? A question that continued to resonate with me as I navigated through the pages of the three volumes. "There is a moral to this story hidden in plain sight – not everyone who is fighting for you, may believe in your human right".

When you read about the establishment of the 'Apprenticeship Laws', you cannot but think about the current state of our child welfare system – "So come and give me your children I will make them apprentice, For you cannot even care for them and that fact hurts my conscience". You read about the 15th Amendment and the provision of voting rights. But you also learn about the introduction of the poll tax that prohibited many Black people from not only voting and having their voices heard but also denied them hope and choice.

Enslaved – A Chronicle of Resistance comprises of three volumes – The Lamentation of the Enslaved (set between 1700-1800), Freedom Bells are Ringing (1800-1900) and Hidden in Plain sight (present day). The volumes are connected by a very powerful refrain from the Kingdom of Nri (Nigeria), a kingdom of freedom and haven for marginalized peoples. "I am child of the Kingdom of Nri, We believe ALL men are born to be FREE. This gift is granted by Chukwu to all, That enter into Nri's great hall". We are all born FREE. And plainly we are all free where we live today. However, hidden in plain sight are many shackles, chains, constraints, limitations, barriers, and abuses.

Brain Sankarsingh brings these hidden and ongoing issues to the forefront through amazing poetic literature introduced by thought provoking and context setting introductions. One cannot but enjoy his work. – **Liben Gebremikael, Executive Director TAIBU Community Health Centre**

Table of Contents

Foreword i
Dedications iii
Acknowledgements v
About the Cover vii
About Capitalizations and Language Conventions viii
Introduction ix
A History Lesson – The Beginning 1
The Land Speaks 5
Humanity's Mourning 7
Mufa 9
eguzogidela 12
Helpless Cry 15
Mufa's Identity 17
The Ocean's Breath in His Ear 20
I am John Brown 23
Mufa's despair at sea 26
Into the cauldron 28
Mufa's Loss 30
John Brown 39
Winter of His Heart 41
Stripped! 43
I Am Human 46

The Auction I	49
The Auction II	52
Broken not Crushed	54
A Song of Remembrance	56
For The Sake of Africa	59
I am the Golden Magnolia	61
I am Samuel Alford III	64
I am Tom	65
My name is Mufa	68
Conversation with Massa	70
Tricked & Stolen	74
The North Star to Freedom	78
Samuel Alford III	79
A Changed Young Girl – Part I	81
Freedom	83
Clemency	86
A Changed Young Girl – Part II	89
Hidden Love Part I	92
Into the night	97
Hidden Love Part II	98
A love letter from Preston to Feewar	101
Feewar's Final Promise	103
Caught!	105
The Golden Magnolia	107

The Wisdom of Samuel Alford III - Colossians 3.22	109
Dear Massa	111
Mufa's Last Thoughts	116
Mufa's Journey – A Retelling	117
Appendix 1 – Flyer of an escaped enslaved	121
Table of Figures	123
Biographies and Poems	124
Brian Sankarsingh	124
Janet L. Wheat-Kaytor	126
J. E. Rehel	127
Loretta Laurie Fisher	128
Sherman K Francis	129
Index	131

Foreword

I reiterate, at the outset, that I am extremely impressed with the general work and the power that flows off the page. It brings to mind – by virtue of its stridency, courage and creativity – some of the writings of authors like James Baldwin, Maya Angelou, Lorraine Hansberry, George Jackson (whose 'Prison Letters' I was privileged to read, in my very early teens, very many moons ago.)

The inclusion of historical fact, with division into three distinct eras, is ingenious. It accurately mirrors the seminal research done by the Caribbean's foremost economist and developmentalist, the late Lloyd Best and Canadian thinker Kari Levitt viz., the Plantation Economy (Pure Plantation, Plantation Modified & Plantation Further Modified – the latter corresponding to the current era). ENSLAVED focusses precisely on these eras, through a more personalized, dramatic, poetic lens.

The accurate portrayal of pre-slavery Africa and its economic and socio-political structures is another case in point. Detailing the horrors of the Slave Trade and the singularity of its profit maximization motive also enhances the work's historical accuracy. As does treatment of 'the white man's burden" – civilizing savages.

The roles of religion and systemic (institutional) racism in facilitating system perpetration and perpetuation, are also well recognized and presented. Well done!

There is a lot more that can be said about Enslaved, A Chronicle of Resistance, all of it complimentary. It would be great to see it added to the existing corpus of relevant literature, and it certainly has my best wishes.

James Baisden (*12-04-1957 - 15-03-2023*)
Educator, Author, Music Producer and Artist

Dedications

I am not a Black person, nor do I identify as a Black person. I am, however, a Person of Colour, and I do identify with the struggle of BIPOC peoples.

This book, therefore, is dedicated to Black people, Indigenous people, and People of Colour everywhere and to their continued resistance of White supremacy – **Brian Sankarsingh**

***

I would like to dedicate this book to our readers and everyone dealing with racism. To my family and friends who support me and love me no matter what, Tony, Nick, and Jeff, you have my heart. To my best friend, Shelley. To the rest of my family, Joy, Rebecca, Jessalyn, and Cheryl, and to my incredible boss Alexey, and co-worker Nina, my extended family – **Janet L. Wheat-Kaytor**

***

My poetry is dedicated to my African Ancestors. Their voices clearly echo through mine. Our heartfelt connection is rooted in systemic oppression which gives fuel to on-going resistance throughout the ages. I appreciate them for wildly cheering me on with the same love and support as my daughters, Leah, Shawna,

Maya, and my grandson, Nathaniel. I also appreciate the encouragement of all my comrades at W.A.C, P.A.C and Spring Socialist Network. Special appreciation for my writer siblings: Brian, Sherman, Janet, and Jason, who forged bravely into wicked storms on this epic journey. Last, but not least, my poetry is dedicated to all humans in the process of finding a true path to freedom – **Loretta Laurie Fisher**

***

My contribution to this beautiful work of art is dedicated to my wonderful and supportive wife of twenty years, Lisa. To my children, Isaiah, Jovan, Jedidiah and Jazara, and to the readers. Be inspired to be advocates for the disenfranchised – **Sherman K. Francis**

***

I dedicate these small lyrical contributions to all people and beings who have sought and who still seek freedom from oppression, tyranny and fear. Furthermore, I would like to dedicate this shared collection of work to all who will read it seeking to come away with more understanding, love and shared desire for change in their hearts. This book is for you. Welcome – **Jason E. Rehel**

Acknowledgements

Without the support and perseverance of my beloved wife and life partner this book would not be possible. It is her strength and optimism that has fueled my own passion for this writing. She is my muse; encouraging, supporting and inspiring me to pursue this crazy dream.

Researching and writing this book was emotionally draining! I am thankful for my friends Hari, Zee and Kris - thank you brothers, for being there and giving me your support when it was sorely needed. Special thanks to Roberta Shaffer for her editing services.

The idea for Enslaved, A Chronicle of Resistance was conceived in the summer of 2020 as I prepared to launch my first book. It began as a seed, and I realized that it would be a severe injustice to tend to it on my own. So started the search for likeminded gardeners. There were several failed attempts, and with each failure, my desperation grew. Then suddenly, in the space of a few weeks, this talented group of poets came together.

I am grateful for the diversity of this team. Each of these poets have had to struggle with this work. Some from a BIPOC perspective and others from a White perspective. We had countless difficult discussions about racism, prejudice and hate. But every one of those discussions ended with a deeper understanding and empathy on both sides.

About the Cover

Under cover of darkness, in the chill of the night, a figure looks up to the sky. He tries to find the North Star. For him this star is a beacon of freedom. He does not know how to read or write; but he has memorized the night sky and the North Star in particular. This star would be his guide as he secretly travels about 800 miles due north. This star is the symbol of his freedom.

We hope, dear Reader, that as you read these poems, **Enslaved** becomes your North Star. We hope that you are challenged to address systemic racism and its equally dangerous opposite woke nihilism in all their sinister forms, and that your own stories will one day become poems.

About Capitalizations and Language Conventions

In this book, Enslaved, A Chronicle of Resistance, the poets have agreed to capitalize Black and White when referring to racial groups.[i] In the current climate of hate, demonization and polarization, we feel it is better to build bridges. This does not mean we diminish or ignore history; after all it is the path that brought us to this place. We risk much more than division between races if we choose to ignore history. We risk our humanity.

We use Canada English conventions in the book.

Introduction

Enslaved, A Chronicle of Resistance is the first modern book of its kind.

It is a chronicle of enslavement and resistance told in an exquisite blend of prose and poetic verse. Through the esthetic rhythms and rhymes of poetry, it chronicles the establishment and institutionalization of systemic racism. Each poem tells its own story, but each is also part of a bigger narrative. A story, within a story.

A prelude to each poem sets the context and moves the story along. Some of these preludes describe the historical, cultural, societal, political or economic environment as well.

Enslaved, is not just poetry about the atrocities of African slavery and the horrible price humanity continues to pay for it. Neither is it just a story of racism, bigotry, discrimination or prejudice. It is a story about dominion, power and control. It plunges the depths of depravity humanity can sink to and the things they are willing to do to justify it all. It is also a story of hope, courage and optimism as can only be told through poetry. It powerfully tackles the subjects of racism, Shadeism (the discrimination against an individual based on their skin tone), the use of racist symbols and systemic racism in a time when the world is caught up in debate as to what all of that really means. It shows the birth of systemic racism and challenges readers to address it in whatever colour it rears its head.

As humanity stands on a precipice, looking down into the darkness of its own historical hate and racial prejudice, Enslaved, A Chronicle of Resistance, reminds them of past horrors, before challenging them to step back from the precipice.

The United Nations sees slavery as an umbrella term that is related to forced labour, debt bondage, forced marriage and human trafficking[ii]. In other words, any situation(s) of exploitation that a person cannot refuse or leave because of threats, violence, coercion, deception, and/or abuse of power.

Sadly, for as long as humans have wandered the face of this blue planet, some have hungered to exercise dominion over others. This heartless need to dominate and rule over those perceived to be "lesser" or "sub-human", has corrupted and contaminated humanity throughout history. Our conquered enemies become our slaves for life. We demand servitude as payment for debts, real and imagined. Whole clans and tribes serve only as fodder for would-be landowners and royalty because of perceived status.

From the cave to the pyramid, castle to tenement, the hunger to dominate another's life has beleaguered us. When driven by the need to occupy the top of the food chain, many are all too willing to stand upon the lifeless bodies of their fellow human beings.

One practice, however, stands head and shoulders above it all. It is the one that serves as a lesson in what happens when one race uses all its resources, power, abilities and even the moral authority of its religion to rule over another.

The depraved cruelty of the American enslavement trade has eclipsed all other known examples. However, we must acknowledge that a simple reason we are so keenly aware of the atrocities of the American enslavement of Africans is that it is well documented. We have historically accurate records that describe the brutalities done to the African enslaved people. There are court cases where enslavers were tried for killing the enslaved and more recently, historically accurate non-fiction books – and later movies – that use

enslavement as the backdrop of storytelling. These have all served to help preserve Black history.
These series of books walk a fine line between historical fact, fiction and our present reality. The poets acknowledge that they did not write about every single Black person or Person of Colour who resisted enslavement and their ongoing struggle against systemic racism. There were, and continue to be, so many brave and resilient people who engage in this fight. Without their struggle we would all lose; if they are not mentioned here, that does not diminish their contributions.

The story is divided into three books and one companion reader.

> **Book 1 - The Lamentation of the Enslaved** set between the 1700s to the mid-1800, examines the beginning of African enslavement and plunges into the pain and struggle of several enslaved Africans. This is the time of enslavement – the exercise of absolute power of one race of people over another. Where Blacks are bought, sold and owned as personal property and White people exert dominion over them and the fruits of their free labour.

Book 2 - Freedom Bells are Ringing set between the mid-1800s and 1900s is the book where, at first, hesitantly and cautiously the newly freed Enslaved, celebrate freedom only to realize that the ringing of the freedom bell was a hollow unfulfilled promise. In this book, we see the continuation of enslavement in other crueller ways. Slavery was perpetuated through the systems of segregation and Jim Crow. The book, celebrates the lives and struggles of stalwarts like Harriet Tubman, Robert Smalls, W.E.B Dubois, Frederick Douglass, Viola Desmond, Malcolm X and Martin Luther King Jr.

Book 3 - Hidden in Plain Sight explores systemic racism in the modern day. It describes yet another evolution of enslavement. All the old accoutrements, language, symbols and memories of the past have been challenged and some have been rooted out and destroyed. However, one mechanism is left to dismantle – systemic racism. It is the spectre of racism that is hidden in plain sight.

Book 4 - A Companion Reader is written as a companion to books 1 to 3 and allows the reader to read about the historical context without poetry. It references the poetry by book and according to chapter content.

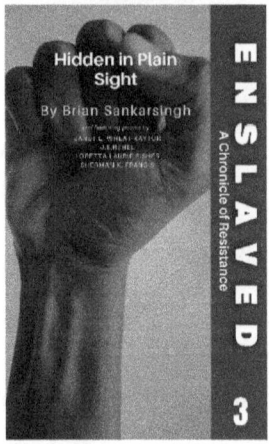
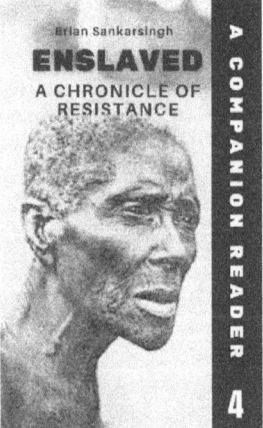

BOOK 1

THE LAMENTATION OF THE ENSLAVED

Figure 1-The Lamentation of the Enslaved

A History Lesson – The Beginning

Although the beginning of slavery is shrouded beyond the mists of antiquity we know that it has been around for as long as we have kept records. While many modern minds recognize the innate repulsiveness of the practice, we must accept its existence and the fact that it continues to exist in our time.

Slavery dehumanizes. It violates the rights of the individual by denying them their freedom. It degrades them to a form of property to be bought, sold or traded at the will of the enslaver. It makes them into livestock. Slavery exploits the labour of the individual and returns no economic, social, political or financial gain to the enslaved. Slavery thinking assumes that one is lesser and another better, and the lesser is blessed by serving the better.

But how do we differentiate between lesser and better?

Slavery has always existed, this much we know is true
From the pyramids of Egypt to the land of Timbuktu
Serf, vassal, servant, bondsman and many other names

The Lamentation of the Enslaved

Call it what you want, the principle is still the same
The unlucky ones among us, disenfranchised and the poor
Have always been the first, forced through slavery's door

Peering into the hallowed halls of antiquity
We are confronted with slavery's grim reality
People bound by chains that are not always physical
To enslavers who sometimes, are not always tyrannical
What we know is that one human sees himself as better
 And he is more than willing, to enslave another

Through a perverted lust for power and untold rapacity
Many Empires used human slaves with extreme veracity
But nothing else comes as close to unholy morality,
Than the evil personified in American slavery
This was very different from what was seen before
Its dark abiding heinousness would change the world forevermore

> *America's history with enslaving African people started long before August 1619[ii] and to not acknowledge that would be to ignore*

> *the savagery and barbarity visited upon people of African descent. August 1619, however, is viewed as a turning point in the emergence of slavery in America.*

What started in Jamestown, Virginia in sixteen hundred and nineteen[iii]
Would become the most gluttonous monster the world had ever seen
Twenty enslaved Africans would be traded for merchandise
Eventually opening the floodgates, from which there was no reprise
America became addicted to the drug of free African labour
In due course, that addiction would become its nadir

First, they were used as labour to farm rice, tobacco and indigo
Until Eli Whitney invented the cotton gin,[iv] it was no longer status quo
The gin made it easier to produce cotton in greater quantities
Increasing the demand for slaves from America to the colonies

The Lamentation of the Enslaved

Over twenty million[v] souls would eventually be stolen and sold
Voracious plantations consumed them with an appetite uncontrolled

***

The Land Speaks

Humanity always seems to be at odds with itself. Showing vitriolic hate in one instance and tremendous loyalty, love and forgiveness in another. This dichotomy has permeated our existence. It has stained the land with rivers of blood pitting brother against brother. It has even influenced how we govern ourselves.

What if the Earth itself could speak of all it has seen? What would it say about the brutality of our wars? What would it say about the destruction of life in the pursuit of dominance over life? How would it cry for the rivers of needless blood washing over it? What would it think about the savagery, vileness and brutality visited upon enslaved Africans?

If I could fail to yield the fruits
That makes the cruel rich
What joy would be mine, though
I could not share them with those I care
I feel the pain and soak up blood and tears
That drips from the burdened brow

The Lamentation of the Enslaved

I see the whip drawn and desire to warn
But within me, such power doth not lie
My bowels have cradled those
That sleep the sleep of death
And I dream of arms to comfort the living
That so desperately need it
As the enslavers walk my stomach churns
To open and their souls devour
For how can one, with similar frame
Treat its kind with utter disdain

The colour of skin doesn't change the substance
I reclaim at your life's journey's end
Hence, I long to see compassion's day
When skin no longer defines
And one is judged by the heart's abundance
For within true humanity resides
So, for now I may be the only one
Who treats all with equality
I give my yield to all and sundry
From all that lies within me

***

Humanity's Mourning

As the Earth laments the evils of slavery, we mourn for Africa. There is a certain cruel irony that this land, the birthplace of humanity, is where such heinous evil was perpetrated against humanity. The pain, savagery and ruthless atrocities would cripple Africa forever. A once-prosperous land, brought to its knees by stealing its people, despoiling its flora and fauna and plundering its resources and treasures.

Let us lift up a song to humanity's birthplace.

O People, let us sing of Africa, the cradle of humanity
She intended all her children to share equality

> *O people mourn for Africa the cradle of humanity[vi]*
> *Grieve for her people, who have been subjected to slavery*

Sing of her verdurous land from jungle to savannah
Flourishing and luxuriant in Nature's panorama

Teeming with life, reflecting her bountiful glory
From Mount Kilimanjaro to the wondrous Serengeti

The Lamentation of the Enslaved

Sing of the animals freely roaming the grasslands
Unbeholden to anything but Nature's own commands

In the circle of life, each one plays their role
From the proud and stately lion to the newborn foal

> *We weep for our teeming wildlife hunted for skins and ivory*
> *Slaughtered for no other reason than their petty thievery*

Sing of her rainy season and the landscape lush and green
Of her amazing vistas still untouched and still pristine

> *We weep for those dear ones, men women and children*
> *Kidnapped from her bosom, stolen by the millions*

Sing of her stalwart men, strong as the Baobab tree
Her women are the epitome of grace and exotic beauty

> *We weep for the decimated tribes, men and women gone*
> *Stolen from their motherland, never to return*

O people mourn for Africa the cradle of humanity
Grieve for her people, who have been subjected to slavery

***

Mufa

Our story begins with Mufa, Abimola's son. He is a strong, lithe young man. His beautiful black skin shimmers in the brilliant African sunshine. Mufa's father, Abimola, was born in the Nri kingdom[vii]. Nri is a kingdom within the Igbo area of Nigeria. It exerted significant political and religious influence over Igboland.

Nri was ruled by a priest-king whose title was Eze-Nri and who was seen as having divine authority in religious matters.

The kingdom of Nri is a haven for people who had been removed or rejected by their communities. It is a place where slaves are set free and people in bondage are given their liberty. Ironically, the Atlantic trade of enslaved people was one of the reasons for Nri's eventual decline in the 18th century. If ever there was a civilization lost for humanity to mourn, it would be that of the kingdom of Nri.

Mufa is a true child of Nri. He understands the brutality and inequality of slavery and why humanity must shun it. The spirit of Freedom occupies every bone in his body. Since childhood Mufa was taught about the importance of free will and the malevolence of slavery.

I am Mufa
Abimola's son
From the Kingdom of Nri[viii]
Ruled by the anointed Eze Nri
Our kingdom is a theocracy

Eze Nri has divine authority
Our people have always been free
We reject all forms of slavery
This is how we built our community
We believe in peace and decency

Our first and blessed king, Eri[1]
Was in his own right, legendary
He established a peaceful society
In the Anambra River valley
Sent by Chukwu[2] himself to be
The first leader of the Kingdom of Nri

---

[1] Eri is said to be the original legendary cultural head of the Umu-eri groups of the Igbo people
[2] Chukwu is the Supreme Being of Igbo spirituality

I
Am
Mufa!

***

The Lamentation of the Enslaved

eguzogidela

(*Pronounced Egu-uzo-gid-ela – 4 syllables*)

Abimola warned Mufa about 'the kidnappings'. There were rumours that the people who were abducted were taken to a new land, but no stories of what happened to them after that. Abimola knew he could not stop his son from hunting and foraging, but demanded he always be aware of his surroundings.

One fateful day, however, coming back from a day of fruitful hunting, Mufa happened upon some villagers. This chance encounter would change the entire trajectory of his life. Nothing would ever be the same again. As he struggled to escape, one of the men tells him to stop fighting. In Igbo, eguzogidela means resist not or don't resist.

Igbo[ix] is one of the official languages of Nigeria and in the Kingdom of Nri. It is spoken in the Southern Delta states of Abia, Anambra, Ebonyi, Enugu, and Imo, as well as in the northeast of the Delta state and the southeast of the Rivers state.

People who were captured were taken to a holding area called a barracoon[x]. A barracoon was a type of barracks or small enclosure where captured Africans were temporarily held to then be shipped across the Atlantic Ocean. People were held in these barracoons until a ship was available. This could take days or months. Many Africans died in these barracoons.

What?
How could he tell me to stop fighting?
With brawny arms around my neck slowly tightening
The air around me swimming
My vision quickly dimming

I awake to the putrid smell of fear and trepidation
Slowly washing over, me, a terrible realization
Then from behind the clouds peeped Old Father Moon
Confirming my deepest fear - I was in a barracoon

Sweat and panic in my throat form a silent scream
Just to reassure me, this was not a dream
Cries from shapeless forms, punctuate the silence
I make an unvoiced promise to be ever defiant

The Lamentation of the Enslaved

Stories of the missing children, women, men
Taken to a foreign land, seized by the White demon
Stubbornly I fight off sleep, to show no sign of weakness
I am Mufa, Abimola's son, I whisper to the darkness

Sunshine gently awakens me from my sleepy cocoon
Shaking away that terrible dream, of the barracoon
Silence shattered by a cracking whip, a scream that makes me swoon
This was no dream, this terrible barracoon

As the sun rose in the sky, I understood my plight
The horrors of the place no longer hidden by the night
Others like me sit in silence, emptiness in their eyes
In heart-breaking acceptance of their ultimate demise

I feel the bite of hunger as the dewy morning falls away
It fuels my desperation as my mind hunts for an escape
What do they intend to do with us, what could be their plan?
All I know is that our troubles started with the coming of the White man

***

Helpless Cry

Can any one of us say that we understand the pain the enslaved Africans had to bear? Time has removed us from the horrors they endured. It may have lessened the hurt, but the impact of the brutality, savagery and cruelty visited upon the enslaved is visible even today. This pain has reverberated through the centuries and had adverse effects on all their descendants.

Day by day I scream for help in tones
that cannot be heard
My cries go unseen though written in
bold across my face
My father provided shelter to
all who did seek it
But there is no haven for me,
one who so desperately needs it!

Time after time I see the land
the groves I long to roam
I smell the trees and taste the air
that once my cheeks caress
This precious land that I call home

The Lamentation of the Enslaved

for safety, many did flee
Yet for me and my constant plea
I find no sanctuary

Moment by moment a familiar sound
awakens my attention
I look up to find that in my mind
will be its forever home
My people showed compassion
and in persecution offered refuge
Yet I find no one to deliver
me from my affliction

From sun to moon and then again,
the scenes play on repeat
The familiar voices call me back
to nature's calm retreat
Our humble home was a resting place
to many needing rescue
Who to hear me when I call
and a hand of solace extend?

***

Mufa's Identity

Even while waiting for the arrival of the ship, slaves were expected to earn their keep. Here they would get a taste of what their future lives would be like. Whether it be the threat of violence or withholding of food, they were forced to obey.

At first, Mufa tries to stand his ground, after all, he is a child of Nri. Slavery is anathema to his worldview. It is not too long, however, until he too is broken.

My name is Mufa
And I am 16 years old
I am in what's called
A "barracoon"
To me it is a small enclosure – but might as well be called a cage

When I left home, I was strong and had a good heart
I loved my family, and I helped support them
I would do anything for anyone

The Lamentation of the Enslaved

I have been in this barracoon for so long now
The goodness in my heart and my soul
Has disappeared deep within
I see goodness in no one
      not anymore

Every day men leave and come back with cuts on their faces,
their bodies looking broken
I am told that food is used as a reward for doing these men's bidding
they starve them until they listen,
then feed them a piece of bread,
a piece of meat

One day I was asked to do something and stood my ground and said 'no'
I was taken out of the barracoon and crushed
stepped on and beaten
I returned with a black eye that I could hardly see out of

I was limping
and I remained hungry for what seemed like an
eternity until I was asked again to do something
and I complied
> time after time.

***

The Ocean's Breath in His Ear

How did the enslaved view the ocean that lay before them?

While for years European and other colonizers saw the ocean as an opportunity to increase their wealth and expand their empires and dominion, the enslaved Africans may have looked upon it with trepidation. A blue expansive abyss that had swallowed others before them and now was preparing them for yet another feast.

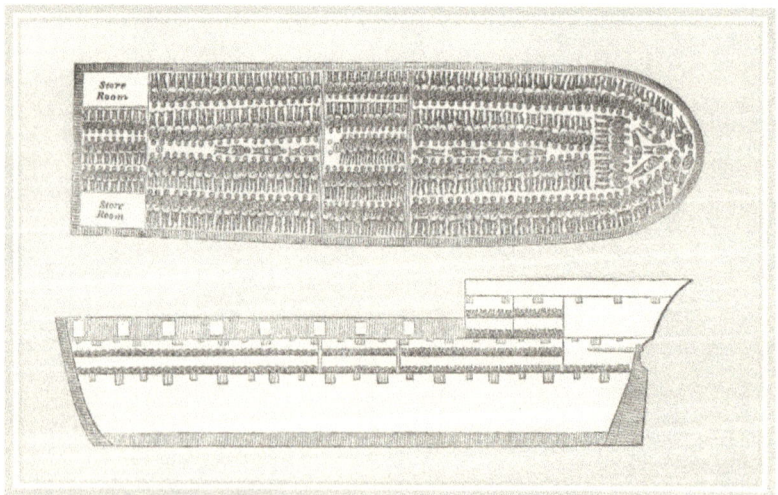

Figure 2 - Slave ship - [[File:HOS D326 Decks of a Slave Ship.jpg|HOS D326 Decks of a Slave Ship]] Blake, William O, Public domain, via Wikimedia Commons

The ocean's breath was never sweet, even in his dreams
It carried currents of bad weather
whispered harsh outlines of colonial schemes
Pulled and pushed to the shore's tether
The infinite pale whale's jaws of open waves awoke
within him a shame
One he never knew existed, a fear newly persistent
without even a name

No pain yet to claim

And oh, how he yearned for the calm still of Nri's lake
the gentle breezes carrying birdsong and hunters' cries
back home
Time stood still back then at the tops of trees, and
longer did it make

the current moment and its unnatural horrific lies
landing around him like stones
"What can be their purpose, what can be this evil's
aim?"
he dared not wonder aloud anymore among the tides,
amid horns' drones

The Lamentation of the Enslaved

Back in his village, his nation, his family recited the same
It's the salt, not the water; it burns, it doesn't quench him
It's the corner, before the blindside; it's not a gateway to redemption
It's where evolution made a great burst; where here it's bent on the reverse
Just to leave him, and millions more
With centuries of thirst
Lonely on the shores,
those whose bones
weren't neatly dissolved;
In the supremely White foams,
Of Atlantic indifference
Erased from history's manifests
Through the will and the chosen destinies
of America's OG White supremacists

***

I am John Brown

John Ignatius Brown was not the typical ship captain. He worked his way up to owning his ship by being shrewd and discrete – at least that was the story he told himself and everyone willing to listen to him.

He had dropped his middle name early on in his life and by doing so dropped the last hold his father had on his life. Ignatius Clement Brown was an alcoholic whose addiction almost ruined his family. John had to learn how to survive on his own; and it was this relentless will to succeed that served him so well. It made him into a hard, phlegmatic man obsessed with money. He would sell his child if it would bring him some profit.

He was especially envious of the plantation owners. He believed that although they dressed in fancy clothes and put on airs - deep down, they were no different from him.

The Lamentation of the Enslaved

Over the years, he had come to expect that some of the enslaved Africans would die during the journey. To maximize his profit, he would pack his ship with as many enslaved as possible. His ship's hold was well ventilated[xi] as he realized that it helped keep his "cargo" healthy.

My name is John Brown, and I can provide
All the slaves that you ever need
Give me your requirement, it will be supplied
In the best of health guaranteed

It's my job to find them and bring them to you
It costs thirty-five pounds for a buck[3]
I have the wherewithal, the ship and the crew
It's a matter of skill not of luck

I've been doing this job since I was a lad
I can supply you with the best
I was on the Clotilde, but not the Amistad[xii]
I would never allow such unrest

---

[3] As part of the animalization of African men they were called "bucks"

On my ship, I am captain and the master
Thereon no mutiny will I abide
Indeed, I am a very hard taskmaster
A duty I conduct with enormous pride

***

The Lamentation of the Enslaved

Mufa's despair at sea

Mufa is shackled and loaded into the ship's hold. With fear and uncertainty on his mind, he did not have time, opportunity or privilege to be in awe of the vast ocean and the extremely large vessel he was forced onto. Deep in the ship's hold packed tightly and chained with all the others, he cannot, even in his wildest imaginings, know what is in store for him.

As the ship leaves the dock, he knows that something ominous is happening. The journey would take about a month at sea. In earlier journeys, some of the slaves threw themselves overboard preferring to die than continue the torture. Because of this, John Brown ensured that they were kept shackled as much as possible.

Oh, the smell is making me sick
Is it the movement?
The grip of hunger?
The lingering pain of the whip?
We're packed so tightly in this place
There's hardly room to breathe

The salty air mixed with fear
A miasmatic smell that fills the air

Where are they taking us?
What are they going to do with us?

I look for consolation in
The faces of my fellow prisoners
Lost
Bewildered
Fearful
Defiant
Broken
Sad
Hateful
Black sweaty faces
Some with dull lifeless eyes
In death's warm embrace
Someone just vomited
The stench makes me gag

***

Into the cauldron

Many of the enslaved drowned as they tried to escape the ships traversing the Middle Passage. Driven mad with the need to escape and be free they chose to leap overboard at the first chance they got.

To leap into a cauldron without really knowing what to expect; only sure of one thing – they were no longer on that boat to nowhere.

I
    Must
        Escape

Jump
    Splash

Enveloped in a watery womb
I try to stand
With no ground beneath me
I try to float
My body weighed down and heavy

Breathe in
Air
Sucked under I breathe in
Water
Salt burning my nose and throat

I hear people screaming above
Seeing
Waterlogged forms
One
More
Breath and
    I am
        No
            More

                ***

The Lamentation of the Enslaved

Mufa's Loss

We have all lost someone and, in that loss, we go through several stages of grief. The person who was dehumanized and dragged into the hold of a ship sailed across the Middle Passage and into a foreign land lost many things. They lost their identity, their humanity, their dignity, their home and their family.

Elisabeth Kübler-Ross described several stages of grief and loss[xiii]. She recognized that even though people come from different walks of life, diverse cultures and lived experiences they all have something in common at some point in their lives – loss and grief. This was no formula but a range of emotions a person might experience as they went through a traumatic loss.

When he was in the barracoon, Mufa may have still entertained some belief that he would be rescued. He could still feel the land of his home, under his feet. He could smell the familiar scent of home on the evening breeze that swept through the barracoon. He was still home. But, as he was forced into the belly of the ship, he begins to understand his dilemma; and as each week of his journey across the Middle Passage stretched on, he realizes there was no rescue coming. The journey is a dull razor that slowly shreds every contact he has with his homeland.

Dear reader, this poem also has section notes – in italics - that give you context about Mufa's experience. Whether you choose to read the section notes and then the verse or ignore the section notes completely is up to you. However, take the time between each verse to imagine the horror the enslaved person was experiencing.

Thrown into the ship's hold, Mufa experiences all these stages of grief as he is rocked to and fro by the vast ocean.

Week 1 - Denial

Mufa is upset. He should have known better, he tells himself. How could he be caught unawares like this? He was aware that people were being taken. Kidnapped never to be seen again. He knew and still allowed himself to be caught. As he sat and waited in the barracoon for an interminable amount of time he had time to reflect and kick himself for getting caught. He

The Lamentation of the Enslaved

replays the events that brought him here all he can focus on is the weight of the man on top of him. Holding him down and tying his arms behind his back. "Eguzogidela!" he loudly whispered. "Do not resist!"

Caught
Like a rabbit in a trap
Herded
Like a cow in a pen
I will not let them break me
They will never take me
From my home, my land
I will fight them with all my might
Beat me and chain me, but
I will not give up the fight

Week 2 – Anger

Bound in heavy chains, Mufa is dragged with his fellow prisoners into the hold of John Brown's ship. In the belly of this beast, Mufa is beginning to realize that no one is coming to save him. He sees the realization mirrored in the eyes of the older men and it frightens him. As the ship slowly begins its journey his fear turns to anger.

> *In the depth of his anger, he calls out to Chukwu[xiv] himself – Chukwu, the Great Being and The Being that creates - asking Him for an opportunity to kill the captain, John Brown.*

I grow nauseous with these waves
The sickly smell of salt in the air
The stench of sticky sweat
Mixed with bodily waste
And death
This is no womb
It is a burial pit, a tomb
Hunger pangs burn my brain
I must escape this dreadful ship
So I can be free once again
I hate this man John Brown
He smells of tobacco and disease
He says I belong to him now
Chukwu[1] grant me a chance to kill him
This I beg of you please

Week 3 – Bargaining

> *Time begins to blur for Mufa as he turns his reflections to his home. He had just entered adulthood when he was taken and lost all the privileges of a young man in*

his tribe. He makes oblations to Amadioha - the aspect of the Great Being Chukwu who brings justice, love, peace, and unity. In a final act of desperation, he reaches out to the ancestors.

Amadioha[2] what did I do to offend you
That you simply allowed
Me to get captured
and tortured
You disliked me so much
That you removed me
From your sight
From the cool savannah breezes
From the arms of my lover
They have stolen my birthright
Made me an orphan
Reborn into little
Less than an animal
Help me, ancestors
I promise I will bless you
With a bounty of yams

Week 4 - Depression

The fourth stage of loss is depression. After four weeks at sea, Mufa's will seems broken. He feels the uncaring sea is his most hated enemy. No answers have been forthcoming from his many prayers and in his heart, he realizes the completeness of his loss. His heart now yeans for the calming and familiar voice of his mother as she stirred the morning fire and sang in her beautiful voice.

The ship's womb
Iron umbilical cord
Constricted, around my neck
Waves of amniotic fluid billowing
My surrogate mother, unconcerned
She refuses to sustain me
Instead, she steals my soul
Erases my identity
Hardens me on the inside
Here I find my
Brothers and sisters
Forged in the fires of
Shared labour pains
Here I am nothing
I have lost my tribe
My friends and my love
Mama's singing at dawn
Now forever gone
I grow sick of eating corn and rice
Sick of the smell of dysentery

Oh! Mama!
What is to become of me?

Week 5 - Acceptance

The Middle Passage was quite literally the great divide that slowly and viciously tore the formerly free, now enslaved African from his identity. The enslaved boarded the ship as human beings and, if they survived, disembarked as something little less than an animal. Mufa has had five weeks to reflect on what he has experienced, and what he is experiencing. These thoughts come to him in the full completeness of his realization that his life is no longer his to live.

Abandoned
Orphaned
Alone
I feel the birthing pains
Of my surrogate mother
I hear groans from my siblings
Some are stillborn
Others disabled
All of us mutilated
By chains and
Whips

Our skin is a canvas of
Loathing and aversion
The dead have been thrown
To the gluttonous sea
Not enough to steal us
Our dead bodies
Sacrificed to this heartless mother
Who merrily
Eats her young

> *Mufa experiences all the stages of grief but goes further; for even as he accepts that he cannot do much about the situation he is in, he promises himself that he will not lose who he is. This trait proves to be one that Mufa will pass on to his future family; one that helps them grow strong despite the odds, fight for others around them and remain true to who they really are.*

Week 6 – Defiance

Dragged outside
I feel Anyanwu's[4] light
Amid the cacophony of the wharf
His light gives me succour
He will sustain me

---

[4] Anyanwu (anyaanwū, meaning "eye of the sun" in Igbo) is the sun goddess of the good fortune, knowledge, and wisdom in the traditional Igbo religion called Odinala

The Lamentation of the Enslaved

Even through
this Trial
But they will not break me
Take "me"
    From me
I.
Am.
Mufa!
Abimola's son.
A child of the Kingdom of Nri

              ***

John Brown

Being a mean-spirited and vengeful man who was unafraid to use violence to get his way helped John succeed despite the odds against him. Others might call him a slaver, but John knew he was a supplier, and his product was in high demand. Fuelled by his envy of the rich plantation owners, the enslaved Africans are his best cargo yet.

The smell of my armpits reek to the highest heavens
I wear that smell proudly for it's the way I tell my story
I was born with no silver spoon, there was no inheritance
to help me on my way
my life was a struggle, not a gift or a boon
When you fight for scraps of food, there is no time for play
My father was a drunk who beat me all the time, my mother sold her body to make ends meet. It didn't take me long to embrace a life of crime
That's how you survive the brutality of the streets
The sweat runs down my greasy brow I could hardly give a damn. I did not come here to make friends

The Lamentation of the Enslaved

got no apologies to extend
I started as a deckhand on the Clotilde
in the summer of 1827, I finally found the way to escape
that horrid life. Sailing on the open seas, living
under the heavens. Depending on no one, except my trusty knife
That was when I found my passion
the thing I was good at, a thing many did not want to do
but still in high demand. Capturing and selling slaves
for the rich aristocrats, to work on their plantations
and help them tend their land
I don't care what you think of me, with your sensibilities
You need the slaves that I provide
you and I are undoubtedly allied. You turn your rich noses up at me, but you know that you need me. I don't give a damn about your pride
I'm the one who's facing the many dangers of the sea
While you live in mansions in your precious countryside

***

Winter of His Heart

The ocean represented the knife's edge for the enslaved. Whatever emotions and despair they felt in the barracoon at least they were still on the land they loved. Their home! But here, shackled like animals in the hold of this ship, the despondence, feelings of impending doom and wretchedness would have been palpable.

Out here it's impossible to reason
    heavens never give way to the boundaries of hell
    he can't even divine the season
    instead, stitching moments between each nauseous swell

"O winter of my heart," his spirit leaps in his chest
    The words knot at his throat
    then curdle into anger behind his eyes, a test
    "I will not cry aboard their boat"

His consciousness lingers for days, weeks even,
    Fingers gripping chains intermittently, between shards of dreams

The Lamentation of the Enslaved

    Exalted breaths of salty air are all that's heaved, then,
    In this den of hell at the root of a million screams

From Nri and all he knew they sailed and crashed into infinity
    of pale White horror bent on its own gain and more
    Over the side of the boat, and given to divinity,
    he spilled his spirit of home to preserve something of a core –

Something to carry him onward into the fire
Even seeing the destination ahead and its pit of dire

***

Stripped!

Ship captains did not see the enslaved Africans as human beings. The fact that John Brown ventilated the lower decks was done to ensure that as many as possible of his cargo survived. He made sure that they were under watch so that none would jump overboard to their death. Not because he cared for them but because that would be lost profit.

As the journey wore on, the realization as to the direness of their circumstance, the deplorable conditions of the ship's hold, and depression caused many of them to try and jump overboard. So, although it is estimated that approximately two million slaves died in the journey of the Middle Passage no one knows how many of them died through this form of suicide.

If I'd jumped ship, I'd be at the bottom of the sea but at least - **free**
But I'm now on the auction block stripped of all my God-given dignity!

The Lamentation of the Enslaved

My past, present, and future all ripped from me simultaneously!
Wrongful taking and raping of ancestors and my precious progeny!

My family: snatched from our home, forced into slavery and misery!
Not seen as fully human, merely objects for oppressive cruelty!

European mercenaries grabbed us as trophies to bring their kings and queens
And just like snakes in the grass repeated this low-down scenario for centuries!
United in their venomous scheme to commit transatlantic grand larceny
Addicted to plundering our precious wealth, they decimated African royalty
Additionally denying the excellence of the African Kingdom's existence
Especially those brave warriors who successfully put up a resistance!

As hand-picked targets, my kin have been decreed to feed the greed

of fake masters feigning world ownership and faux racial superiority
If I jumped ship, I could've been floating free at the bottom of the sea!
Instead, I'm for sale on an auction block as a labourer in a field

***

I Am Human

Did every White person who lived during the trade of enslaved peoples support it? If they didn't support it, how did they reconcile the evil that was being perpetrated? Did they even see this as evil or was it just distasteful? In other words, was it something they would never do or something they would never condemn others for choosing to do?

At the heart of it there is only one way of reconciling it all – to internally accept the argument that the Africans were not "real or fully" human. Accepting that, allowed for the treatment they received without compromising the White religious, cultural, and ethical mores.

Mufa asks himself if he gets the opportunity to do so, will he try to escape by jumping into the water? His mind does not quite understand the depth and breadth of the ocean, but he feels that he must do all that he can to survive. Now, standing in a crowded enclosure he hears the murmurs of those around him. This is a market! And they are the produce.

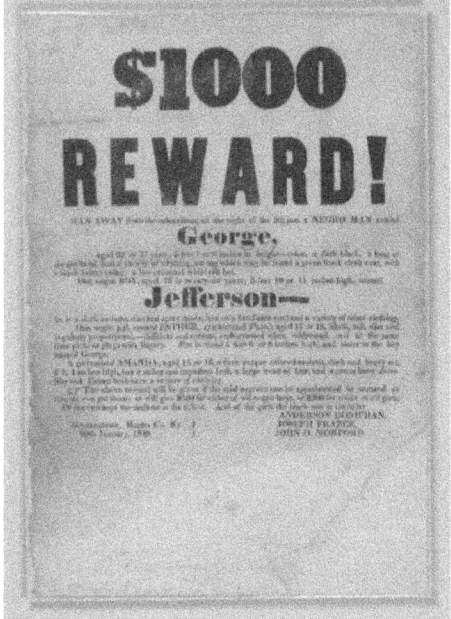

Figure 3 - Runaway slave - Collection of the Smithsonian National Museum of African American History and Culture, Gift from the Liljenquist Family Collection January 20, 1840
See Appendix 1 for a full description of this pamphlet

If I'd jumped ship, I could've been floating free at the bottom of the sea!
But now I'm up for sale on this auction block, as merely a commodity

Stripped of all my God-given humanity
So, a fake master can see every inch of me
And record me as an economic transaction in his-story

The Lamentation of the Enslaved

To shame, monetize and criminalize me

Now, and centuries from now, into future eternity
Although I already have God-given equality and equity
Unfortunately, some plantation owners' progeny has yet to see
That my Black life matters equally among all God's precious humanity and

I am human

***

The Auction I

Slaves would be prepped before going to the auction block. They were brought from the ship to a holding pen and would be oiled or covered in tar to give them a 'healthier look.' They were then branded to show they were slaves. A hot iron was used to sear their flesh as is commonly done with livestock. Next, they would be taken to the auction block.

Auctions were either ones where the enslaved were sold to the highest bidder or what was, at the time called grab and go auctions. The former was comparable to many auctions today; apart from the fact that human beings were being sold. One by one the enslaved would be taken out and displayed. Bidders would poke and prod the enslaved to figure out their state of health. The auctioneer would begin the bidding process and the person who bid the most would be the new owner.

Grab and go auctions were more chaotic affairs. Slave tickets could be bought with each ticket being the equivalent of one enslaved person. People would then line up outside a cage full of slaves and on the beat of a drum would 'grab' the number of slaves they had

The Lamentation of the Enslaved

bought tickets for and leave. The only way an enslaved person could leave the auction compound was by an owner showing a ticket[xv].

As the realization of his circumstances slowly dawns upon him, Mufa is sickened. Under his breath, he whispers to himself, "I am a child of the kingdom of Nri! We believe all men are born to be free. This gift is granted by Chukwu to all that enter into Nri's great hall." Mufa continues to recite this under his breath hoping that it will help him awaken from this horrible dream.

Figure 4 - Selling slaves - American Anti-Slavery Almanac, Public domain, via Wikimedia Commons

Brian Sankarsingh

The smell of death assaults my senses
Shackles bite into my skin
I put up my internal defences
Those still alive are sharing my pain
Where are they taking us, when will we get there
What is to be our fate?
We all look to each other in defiant despair
As we all silently contemplate
We've seen men murdered and our women raped
The first chance we get, we will try an escape
Activity on board the ship has increased
Are we at the end of our journey?
This journey has left so many deceased
That being alive now concerns me
I step into the blinding sun wary as can be
I promise myself that I will run
The minute they take their eyes off me
But the opportunity never arises
We form a line on a block
White men shouting meaningless numbers
As I realize we are no more than livestock
My heart breaks for myself and the others

***

The Auction II

Henry Walton Bibb[xvi] (May 10, 1815, in Shelby County, Kentucky – 1854) was an American author and abolitionist who was born enslaved. He escaped from slavery to Canada, where he founded an abolitionist newspaper called The Voice of the Fugitive. Henry wrote "the most rigorous examination of the enslaved by the inspectors before the sale was on gauging their intelligence.

Intelligence was the most objectionable of all the qualities connected with the life of an enslaved person. Slaveholders believed that when an enslaved Black person is intelligent, "it undermines the whole fabric of his chattel hood; it prepares for what slaveholders are pleased to pronounce the unpardonable sin when committed by the enslaved. It lays the foundation for running away and going to Canada. They also see in it, love for freedom, patriotism, insurrection, bloodshed, and exterminating war against American slavery."

Next on the block, we have
A strong young buck

With many years of service ahead
Use him for breeding, and in the fields
A wonderful addition to your farmstead

100
    125
130
    140
150
    225

Come on gentlemen he's worth more than that
A sound investment for certain
You can't go wrong with this one
Come now who's going to take this bargain

225
    250
300

Going once
Going twice
Sold to the Golden Magnolia

***

Broken not Crushed

If any other race had to endure what the enslaved Africans did - would they still be around? Commingled with stories of atrocities and savagery that was heaped upon them are stories of their perseverance and a resolute will to survive.

Of course, this does not diminish the suffering of Indigenous peoples and other native peoples the world over by the hands of those who saw them as little less than human.

If we are to learn a lesson from this, it would be that we must never allow ourselves to diminish **any** person's humanity.

On his first night on the plantation of his new owner Mufa finally accepts this is no dream. Over and over again, he repeats the rhyme that is now the only thing he has left of his homeland.

"I am a child of the kingdom of Nri! We believe all men are born to be free. This gift is granted by Chukwu to all that enter into Nri's great hall."

Orphaned man
Alone
Abandoned
Deserted in this place
Longing for my home
Doomed never to return

Enslaved to these ghost men
White
transparent
No colour on the outside
Shadowy on the inside
Parasites on my back

You break my body

    Blood
        Sweat
            Tears commingled

Pain burning in every muscle
But you will not break me

***

A Song of Remembrance

Singing is deeply rooted in African culture. Singing was a form of communication. It was a way of expressing deep feelings and strong emotions. Songs were passed down from generation to generation and were an integral part of their oral tradition.

For Mufa, this is a new dirge. One born from his suffering. It slowly replaces all the songs of Nri that he can remember. This song is now his life, and he immerses himself into its sadness. He allows it to surround him like a cocoon.

I sing of my tribe my home and my land
A song of remembrance of endless grassland
Warm breezes fueled by the hot sun above
Oh, how I long for the land I so love

Why did they take me? What is their plan?
Why are they so strange? These deadly pale men
I long for the drought, the dusty parched land
I long for the dust of the dry blowing sand

I can still hear the thunder on a cloudy afternoon
The sweet smell of the rain during the monsoon
I remember the antelope and the baobab tree
I pine for my home the Kingdom of Nri

Why have they stolen me? Why am I here?
How do I get back home? Tell me I pray?
My feet still feel the heat of the burning hot sand
I feel the knots of the spear in my hand

I hear the lion with his deep rumbling growl
My heart skips a beat I know he's on the prowl
The hyena's laughter filled with ironic spite
A reminder to all animals, be wary tonight

I pray for protection
I pray to survive
I pray for my safety
To make it out alive

I am haunted by the journey to this cursed place
Fear beating in my heart salty sweat on my face
We're packed in so tightly I struggle to breathe
Our hearts struggle together in a fight to be free

The Lamentation of the Enslaved

I am sick, I am tired of moving to and fro.
Where are we going? No one seems to know

I pray for protection
I pray to survive
I pray for my safety
To make it out alive

This song of my tribe my home and my land
This song of remembrance of the endless grassland
The warm breezes blow the hot sun above
Oh, how I long for the land I so love

…Oh, how I long for the land I so love

***

For The Sake of Africa

Many studies[xvii] have been done to figure out how Africa suffered from the burden of slavery[xviii]. Most of these studies generally show, had the trade of enslaved Africans not occurred, Africa would not be the most underdeveloped region of the world. These studies also showed that Africa would have a similar level of development to Latin America or Asia. This shows the outcome of four hundred years of slavery, butchery[xix] and robbing a land of its human and natural resources.

All this way forced to endure untold atrocities
As they decide our genocide, we'll fight with ferocity
However long, this mourning period is to go on
Although the pain is strong, we will continue our song
Even working in White fields is still fighting to survive
By any means necessary, we're staying stubbornly alive
Even with no ancestral drums, we'll manifest our melodies
Without rainforest and jungles, we will still plant remedies!
Colonizers brought us to this place, but also want to erase

The Lamentation of the Enslaved

All as one we must brace against their unwelcoming face
And revere Mother Africa's memory, beauty and grace
Keep hope deep in our hearts, and strategize to escape
from heartless captors throwing our bodies to waste
to build empires to make themselves appear great!

Unless displaced Africans put up brave resistance
we will, as they plan, become lost without a trace!
Oceans of tears have already been crossed
Indeed, we've now been stolen, sold, now bought
But hearts united in solidarity will never be lost
If we staunchly refuse to stay broken at any cost

***

I am the Golden Magnolia

The Golden Magnolia plantation is owned by Samuel Alford III where Mufa (Tom), Tattio (Esme), Feewar (Mary) and Preston are slaves. It is a very large estate that grows cotton, rubber, sugar cane and tobacco. The estate house, or the big house, is found on the northernmost edge of the plantation. There is a long boulevard leading up to it lined with stately trees that provide some protection from the heat. Contrastingly, the dusty gravel road reflects the searing heat of the midday sun. The plantation house has six stately pillars spanning from the ground to the two-storey roof. A porch with blazing white balusters surrounds the entire house.

The Golden Magnolia has been a part of the Alford estate for three generations, a fact of which Samuel Alford III reminds his slaves regularly.

I have stood here for many generations
Stately columns standing at attention
Inside and out a paisley white
Visible on even the darkest night

The Lamentation of the Enslaved

The road that leads up to my porch
Lined with the majestic oak
Leads right up to my courtly stairs
Lending to the dignified air

Boasting wood from Brasilia
I am the Golden Magnolia

I have seen seasons come and go
Basking in their illustrious afterglow
Immerse yourself in my architecture
Enjoy the grandeur of my entire structure

Sit and have tea on the balcony
Come enjoy my hospitality
I am a part of the Alford family
Woven into their lives tapestry

Bordered by beautiful begonias
I am the Golden Magnolia

I witness with indifference
The Black people and their ignorance
Standing in perfect equanimity
Of their enforced slavery

Unaffected and regally I stand
For I am the mansion grand
Gaze upon my beauteous design
No other building can outshine

Lose yourself in my ambrosia
For I am the Golden Magnolia

***

The Lamentation of the Enslaved

I am Samuel Alford III

Samuel Alford III is a middle-aged man who, by any standard, has spent a lifetime in relative ease and comfort. He is content in his position as lord and master of the Golden Magnolia. His confidence in his ability to manage his affairs and those of his plantation comes from years of success. Now with the addition of slaves to his workforce, business is booming for Samuel.

Lord and master
In control
Owns his life
Owns his slaves
Life is good

                ...for Samuel

                    ***

I am Tom

Forcing a person to give up their name is to remove from them an essential part of their identity and since the Africans were not viewed as humans they were seen as being elevated from animal to sub-human. Renaming was an easy and efficient way to expunge the enslaved person's individuality. It hammered home the destiny of the enslaved.

Mufa was sold to the Golden Magnolia along with an enslaved girl called Tattio and an older woman, Feewar.

Brought on the vessel Esperanza, Tattio was only 15 years old. Her face is long and exotic. Her eyes are deep black pools. Her experiences of being captured, chained and thrown into the boat affect her deeply. In the barracoon, she is horrified to see the atrocities being visited upon the women by both the captive men and the captors. The fact that she looks much younger than her 15 years helps her to survive without being sexually assaulted.

On the Esperanza, she sees members of the crew come to the hold and drag some of the other girls and women topside and this frightens her. When the women return beaten and dishevelled Tattio helps Feewar care for them. This brings the two women closer together. '

At forty, Feewar is the older of the two women. Her face is etched with the pain and fear she has endured, but she is kind-hearted and quick to smile. She has seen a lot of hard times, but instead of it hardening her, it has increased her compassion for people. Her calming eyes and loving demeanour automatically make her the caregiver on the Esperanza, and when she gets to the Golden Magnolia Plantation, she will inevitably continue this role.

The word massa in this poem is a corruption of the word master which was a term used by the enslaved to refer to their enslavers as they were not permitted to use personal names.

I am Tom, I am massa Samuel's slave
His god brought me to him to serve
Massa Samuel has taught me how I should behave
If I don't, I'll get the beating I'm told I deserve

Brian Sankarsingh

The name my mother gave me is forbidden in this place
A once strong name in the Kingdom of Nri
There is no more "me" because I've been replaced
By the identity massa Samuel's chose for me

But late in the night as I lay on the ground
I whisper my true name in defiance
I will never let them make me forget the sound
In this one thing, I will show no compliance

I dream of freedom in my native land
Of the savannah breeze upon my face
To do as I please, under my command
Oh! How I long to be back in that place

During the day in my role as a slave
I do what I am told must be done
But deep in my heart in a protected enclave
There, I am Mufa, Abimola's son

> *I am a child of the kingdom of Nri!*
> *We believe all men are born to be free.*
> *This gift is granted by Chukwu to all*
> *that enter into Nri's great hall."*

***

My name is Mufa

Mufa was instantly captivated by Tattio. His heart hurt to see her mistreated. On the ride from the market where they were bought, he kept stealing surreptitious glances at her. Mufa did not know it, but many plantation owners discouraged marriage among the enslaved. Samuel Alford III was of like mind. He did not believe that his slaves were fully human and having them marry seemed like an indecent degeneration of the institution of holy matrimony.

Samuel Alford III bid on me
He saw that I was strong
If I did what I was told, I would be
An asset to his plantation
The man took me with him
I am renamed Tom – but that will never be my name

My name is Mufa!

One day I will leave this place and return to my home
For now, I've no choice, so I will do their bidding

But I will always think about escaping, finding a way
home and being with my family once again
Everything is repetitive and I must live day by day
Until I meet Tattio,
and my life forever changes, yet again

> *I am a child of the kingdom of Nri!*
> *We believe all men are born to be free.*
> *This gift is granted by Chukwu to all*
> *that enter into Nri's great hall"*

***

The Lamentation of the Enslaved

Conversation with Massa

Many nights as he lay on the cold hard ground of the wooden hut he shared with two other men, Mufa would imagine having a conversation with Samuel Alford III.

The huts of the enslaved were small, and the floor was usually lined with dirt. Plantation owners did not build these huts for the slaves. They had to build them on their own with scavenged materials. This meant they were generally unstable and did not protect well against the weather.

Bedding usually consisted of straw. It was not uncommon for Mufa to sleep outside on nights when the weather allowed, as these were essentially bad weather dwellings.

The word massa in this poem is a corruption of the word master which was a term used by the enslaved to refer to their enslavers as they were not permitted to use personal names.

Brian Sankarsingh

                        I dream of being free
                                someday!

Free? Free from what you dare say?

                    Free to forge my own destiny

Tom, think about what you're saying, think about it carefully

            How can I work for you and not be paid?

Think of last night where your head was laid
The food you ate and the clothes on your back
That nice little cottage that you call a shack
These comforts I supply money was spent,
And as I recall you haven't contributed one measly cent

      But I was stolen and forced into treacherous travel
      My whole life upended and my future unravelled
Cast below deck like unwanted baggage being shipped
Failure to comply to your every wish gets me whipped
          Chained like a dog there was no way to run

The Lamentation of the Enslaved

        Would you wish that for your own son?

You were brought from the jungle to civilization
I bought you to work on my plantation
Be thankful that you have a roof over your head
In some other place, you would surely be dead
The price I paid; I need to get my money's worth
Your place is in the fields to toil in the dirt

        Massa please, take time to understand
          There is no price for the life of a man
  The travails of birth both our mothers endured the same
  Only your status and wealth have you playing this game
      The pittance you paid can never compensate
For the years of labour, I've contributed to this, your estate

Payback your price and maybe you might be given
A chance at freedom out there where you think it's heaven

    You've said this often, but the price always changes
    If our places switched, you'd say it was outrageous

Watch your mouth, Tom, you're walking near the edge
One day soon I may commit to that pledge
But for now, this conversation is over and done
Now get some sleep, before the morning's dawn

***

Tricked & Stolen

Listening to Feewar, one cannot help but be impressed by her wisdom. As an older woman, she recognizes that she is the **only** support for the young enslaved girls around her. Their surrogate mother, doula and friend. She has seen enough of life to know that this is hell itself and she weeps silently while tending to her people.

Is there any end in sight? No end to this living nightmare?
In over 4 decades of life Feewar never experienced anything to compare!
Kidnapped and trapped in trauma, sickness, mental turmoil, endless fear and confusion
Bound in heavy chains while on stormy seas suffering serious wounds and contusions
that remain unheeded and untreated, leaving stolen people in distress without any illusions
There would be no help, no mercy, and no reprieve!
Even with her eyes shut tight
against the shackles and the futility of the fight increasing terror would not leave

not even in broad daylight!

The counterfeit sun seems to offer some light
but this sun is actually nothing like
the true tropical soul-healing warmth & life-giving light
from where Feewar's family thrived in her beloved home
She squints on deck, hearing anguished cries and groans
Surrounded by her people; tricked, tortured, and stolen!

An unrecognizable sun tells Feewar she is far from home
Chained painfully with others, but still shamefully alone
With the menacing sun embedded in the face of the sky
like a giant eye of a tiger who has caught its' prey alive!

Throughout the long sea voyage of the torturous middle passage
White sailors sexually abused them with actions brutal and savage!
Desperate to unsee and unhear these highly unspeakable inhumane crimes

The Lamentation of the Enslaved

She wonders 'Is our survival upon arrival a dreaded sign, or a hopeful sign?'
'This nightmare is dragging on and on -- Is this finally the end of the line?'

After endless months of brutal captivity across endless seas
Now suddenly appears this strange land of leafless trees
Her captors' express journey's end with excited cheers on deck, Feewar mumbles against the strange atmosphere
But no one else, all shackled from different tribes hears her

Except for young Tattio from her village, also captured and brought here!
Feewar speaks low to Tattio, trying to calm both their fears

Cold ocean waves shake the chained huddled masses to the core
Brought hard to their knees and breaking their hearts even more!
This is not the end of their suffering; it would continue for sure

Even if this foreign land is to be their final burial ground onshore
Even in her fear, Feewar vows to become a warrior waging war
by surviving however possible; helping Tattio and others to endure

The imposter sun stares fiercely as if Feewar's the intruder
It glares like a former friend who has now turned accuser!
She faces false judgement head-on, but vows to stay strong
She prays for her people, now forced like animals to live on in slavery
Prays for her people who must exhibit the utmost bravery
Prays they can put up a united resistance to gain victory
by exposing Truth: 'Africans have always been part of humanity throughout history'

***

The North Star to Freedom

Many escaping enslaved, used the North Star to help them find their way. They found the Big Dipper which was highly visible in the night sky during late winter and spring.

Heavenly guide
Pointing the way
Light in the darkness of despair
Bathed in the sweat
Of anticipation
Fighting forests and vines
Mosquitos and swamps
Desperately seeking
Your divine influence

***

Samuel Alford III

Coming from a sound conservative Christian background, Samuel has a strong moral code. He is tough but fair in his business dealings. His reputation is that of an upstanding good man.

He treats his slaves fairly and in accordance with Colossians 4:1 "Masters, treat your slaves justly and fairly, knowing that you also have a Master in heaven."

He punishes those he has to using Exodus 21:20-21 "When a man strikes his slave, male or female, with a rod and the slave dies under his hand, he shall be avenged. But if the slave survives a day or two, he is not to be avenged, for the slave is his money."

He reconciles Exodus 21:16 "Whoever steals <u>a man</u> and sells him, and anyone found in possession of him, shall be put to death," because he professes to believe that Africans are not fully human.

The Lamentation of the Enslaved

I am the Master of this plantation
These lands, this home has always been mine
It belongs to me and blood relations
Gifted by my God's hand divine

This is the purpose to which I was born
My right is God-given and consecrated
Let all ye God-fearing men now discern
His mighty blessing in my life celebrated

My family name that stands influential, unbowed
Like my father before me, and his father revered
A name upon which much has been endowed
I am honoured to be Samuel Alford the Third

At my side stands my darling, Martha my wife
Like a beautiful queen, in her regalia
Together we have built a beautiful life
On our plantation, the Golden Magnolia

***

A Changed Young Girl – Part I

Laws regulating rape did not apply to Black people. Accusing a White man of rape would inevitably result in severe beatings and rape. Even if the plantation owner did not condone rape, an enslaved person could never accuse a White man.

Much of what we know about the horrors of enslaved African women was told to us by Harriet Jacobs (1813 or 1815 – March 7, 1897). Harriet was an African American writer, whose autobiography, Incidents in the Life of a Slave Girl, was published in 1861 under the pseudonym Linda Brent. Harriet was born into slavery and was sexually harassed by her enslaver. She eventually managed to escape to the free North.

It is well acknowledged that slavery was difficult for the men, but the horrors visited upon women paled in comparison.

The Lamentation of the Enslaved

Tattio was working in the field one day
When suddenly she felt nauseous
The sun – it must be the sun she thought
But it continued day, after day, after day

Feewar came to the young girl to ask what was wrong
The young girl was pale and looked ill
The girl explained what was happening
Feewar's eyes grew wide, and her face grew hard
She knew why this very, very young girl was sick
One of those disgusting, repulsive and filthy enslavers had done this to her!

Tattio was expecting a baby

Notwithstanding where this child had come from
Tattio was excited as she felt her stomach begin to grow
Although she had suffered many atrocities in her young life, she was looking forward to having this baby
Someone to love
Someone who belonged to her!

***

Freedom

How can we really understand the plight of the enslaved? Words can do little justice to describe what the entire ordeal would have felt like. These human beings, treated like animals without a thought as to their suffering.

But we owe it to them to try.

Preston was enamoured by Feewar. At first, he tried to impress her because often the overseer left him in charge. But he quickly realized that this was the wrong approach.

Merciless
Callous
Cold-hearted

Words to describe these ...men ... that keep us hostage
Took away our freedom

I may seem emotionless
Quiet ...uncomplaining

The Lamentation of the Enslaved

But all of us
deep down… are

Strong
Resilient
Brave

My dream is freedom
Freedom from this field
From this hot sun
From pain
From anguish
From suffering

For all of our freedom
To leave here …with beautiful Feewar
To build a home
WITHOUT White people
WITHOUT savages
WITHOUT brutality

To just …. live our lives

I miss home
HOME IS FREEDOM

Will I ever see my home again?

This hot sun
Burns into my brain
And I need... I want... to be free!

One day

It WILL happen

We will be free!

***

Clemency

> This poem was inspired by a true story from the book American Slavery As It Is, Selections from the Testimony of a Thousand Witnesses[xx]. Section 5, titled **Treatment of the Sick** bore testimony to the ill-treatment of slaves. Sarah M Grimke gave testimony on how a White woman who was considered very religious in one breath prayed for forgiveness of her sins and in the other berated and abused a sick a dying slave for not working.

Martha Phillippe Alford is the mistress of the Golden Magnolia household. She understands her husband's importance and goes to great lengths to ensure that his house reflects it.

She rules with a strong hand and is often of the opinion that Samuel is too appreciative of the slaves. When she was married, she came to the Golden Magnolia with her own slaves. She knows they understand her every wish and know how to please her.

Martha, like Samuel, is very religious and often courts visits by itinerant preachers. During these visits, she makes every effort to ensure her family's place in heaven is secure.

Martha Phillipe Alford

Oh, parson, I beg you, tell me how I can please my Jesus
Anything that I must do to avoid the pit of Hell
For truly, such an end would indeed be grievous
Not what I want, at the ringing of my death knell

I love my precious Saviour so, for His many blessings
I know He died for my sins and one day He will return
He had to go to prepare a place, a place for me in Heaven
Until the time that He comes, my heart will forever yearn

With many slaves He blessed me to make my life a comfort
In His name, I govern them with a hand that's strong and fair
I am sure when He comes in heavenly glory triumphant
He will take me to my new home in the air

The Lamentation of the Enslaved

One of her enslaved women
> *Missus, I is not feeling well, I is very sick*
> *I feeling like I 'bout to pass out*
> *Me chest is hurting, me tongue is thick*
> *Me don't know what dis feeling is 'bout*

Martha Phillipe Alford
You horribly lazy slave, lying is the devil's work
Surely you will burn in Hell for breaking God's command
You have life so easy, for you don't have fieldwork
Better get to it, before your very soul gets damned

I don't believe you'd stoop to lying, you ungrateful cur
Tell the kitchen, you will not be eating anything today
Oh, my Lord, I pray of give me strength, my Saviour
As I deal with this thankless and ungrateful slave

***

A Changed Young Girl – Part II

In her book, Incidents in the Life of a Slave Girl[xxi], Linda Brent recounted how as soon as she turned fifteen her master began making overtures toward her.

"O, what days and nights of fear and sorrow that man caused me. Reader, it is not to awaken sympathy for myself that I am telling you truthfully what I suffered in slavery. I do it to kindle a flame of compassion in your hearts for my sisters who are still in bondage, suffering as I once suffered." – Incidents in the Life of a Slave Girl, Linda Brent

Figure 5 - My child - American Anti-Slavery Almanac, Public domain, via Wikimedia Commons

FAST FORWARD 10 YEARS...

Tattio's daughter was twelve years old and
working alongside her in the field
When she saw two men coming toward them
and she KNEW what was coming next
Protectively she hid Patty behind her back
But the men threw her out of the way and
grabbed Patty by the arms and legs

As her daughter screamed in terror
Tattio attacked the men
clawing them
grabbing at them
Shouting for them to put her daughter down.
As they left with Patty, Tattio tried to run after them,
but
Feewar grabbed hold of Tattio and
held her with all her might

After the men were gone, Feewar pulled Tattio close
and both women sobbed
When Patty came back the next day

She was a changed girl
Like her mother had been 10 years earlier
Her eyes were haunted
her demeanour, sad and her body damaged!
Tattio held her softly and Feewar
wrapped them both in her arms and whispered
"Let's try to get through this together
It's going to be okay…. it's going to be okay"
 As Tattio despaired there would be no way to ever get away
Feewar's fuming anger did not stop her from praying
that the next generation might live to see that great day

***

Hidden Love Part I

Samuel Alford III did not believe it was proper for enslavers to sleep with the enslaved and had very strict orders that his overseers ensure that this did not happen.

He encouraged the enslaved to have children in much the same way as he ensured his animals reproduced. This was in keeping with his religious philosophy that the African might look and behave human but was sub-human at best.

The mortality rate of enslaved people was high. To replace losses, plantation owners encouraged their slaves to have children. For women, childbearing started around the age of thirteen, and by twenty they were expected to have four or five children.

To encourage higher reproduction, some slave owners promised women slaves their freedom after they had produced fifteen children. Young women were often advertised for sale as "good breeding stock".

It was at Golden Magnolia
That Tom and Esme met
So much pain and punishment
As the sun rose and set

The field was full of workers
That hot August day
When the 2 were put together
And Tom felt his mind stray

He saw this lovely young woman
The beauty of her eyes
She began to sing so sweetly
It was such a lovely surprise

But then he heard a sound so common
The crack of a long whip
Esme screamed and fell to the ground
And Tom was reminded of the ship

Where everyone was captive
In a large and open space
Some shackled, some tied
Such fear on each and every face

The Lamentation of the Enslaved

He tried to go to Esme
To ensure she was alright
He saw her face was bleeding
And her dark eyes were full of fright

But as he reached to touch her
He heard another sound
A man yelled and rushed towards him
And pushed him to the ground

He was given a very stern warning
He needed to know his place
To keep working or more punishment
He needed to keep up the pace

Work fast – work hard
Is the way that it is
Or you could face death
And freedom was not his

Later in the evening
He saw Esme sneak outside
He followed behind her slowly
Having heard many times that day she cried

He went up behind her
And wrapped her in his arms
He wanted to hold her forever
To keep her safe from harms

Esme looked at Tom
Staring up into his face
He looked down at her lovingly
And held her in his embrace

He told her he would protect her
And professed he was falling in love
He promised they would leave that place
And prayed to all above

Wanting to find freedom
To take Esme and be free
To live their lives together
Happy, with a family

For now, they would try to hang on
To do what they were told
It was the only way to survive
Wanting to be bold

The Lamentation of the Enslaved

Esme said to Tom

I just want to be free

To love and not have it hidden

For all the world to see

***

Into the night

Mufa knew of many of his enslaved brethren who tried to escape. He often thought about it but could not bring himself to abandon Tattio.

I flee
Into the night
Escape is
My only option
I will not bear
This terrible
Yoke

I hide
Within the belly of the swamp
Losing my scent
In its mucky grime
The dogs barking my name
Vicious carnivores
Seeking to devour my flesh

***

Hidden Love Part II

Henry Bibb, in his book Narrative of the Life and Adventures of Henry Bibb, An American Slave[xxii] (1849) wrote

"A poor slave's wife can never be true to her husband contrary to the will of her enslaver. She can neither be pure nor virtuous, contrary to the will of her enslaver. She dares not refuse to be reduced to a state of adultery at the will of her enslaver."

The full moon covers the land with a bright radiance
The stars sparkle in the sky
The Golden Magnolia, with its large trees and a big White house
Seem like the best place in the world ….

Hidden by the trees
Hidden from the large, White mansion…

Lay shacks full of slaves
Men… women… children…
All who know the secrets the house hides

The ugly truths of horror and pain
A place barren of kindness to them

But this one night …standing outside of one of the shacks
Is a beautiful young woman named Esme (or Tattio as she was once known)
She is leaning against a large tree, looking at the stars and the big moon
And missing her home … her family… and she starts to cry

Out of the darkness walks a young man named Tom (or Mufa as he was once known)
He walks up to her and stares down into her eyes… her big, black, luminous beautiful eyes
Which are full of tears… he wipes them away and takes her in his arms
She jumps away, fearful they will be seen

It has happened before – they were caught with their arms around each other
And both were taken and beaten and tortured
The enslaver did not believe they should have happiness or love
Or even companionship

The Lamentation of the Enslaved

But Tom had seen everyone leave in a large wagon,
headed to a party, all dressed to the nines
He pulls her back close to him and professes his love,
telling Esme how she is the only woman
In the world that he loves …that he wants … that he needs
She is the only thing that helps him get through his
day, knowing he will see her after dark
She tells him she loves him
She wishes things could be different
That they didn't have to keep in a secret
That they could share their love with the world
But, alas, they must stay hidden in the light of day

***

A love letter from Preston to Feewar

Relationships with others give people a sense of self-worth. Although the enslavers did not believe that the enslaved were humans, they felt the same way. These relationships could be so strong, it would prevent them from escaping[xxiii].

She came to Golden Magnolia
A smiling but lonely soul
After months of watching her working
Things were starting to take its toll

She sang while she was working
But in the evening, I saw her eyes
She tried to care for everyone
But when they were asleep, I heard her cries

Feewar and I went outside to talk
Under the beautiful night moon
We fell in love so quickly
Those hot summer nights in June

The Lamentation of the Enslaved

We held each other tightly
It was the only emotion I felt
But then one day we were caught
And I was tied outside with a belt

They took me where Feewar could see me
Strapped up on that big old tree
They whipped me many times
For everyone to see

They told me love was not allowed
That I was just a slave
All I was to do was follow the rules
And that I must just behave

But when I went back to the shack
Feewar wiped the blood away
She knew together we belonged
No matter what they had to say

***

Feewar's Final Promise

Contrary to popular opinion, the enslaved did not accept their roles. They fought every step of the way. Jumping off the boats, preferring to drown and doing all they could to escape.

It is torturous trudging across this strange land
What is this horrific plan? As if these cruel chains
Are necessary to add to this overload of pain
Dragging heart and soul to unimaginable depths
In this dark place who will see our death?
 A fiery sun flashes through dark branches against the sky
The birds are free, yet screech with empathy, echoing my cry
The fake sun is lowered, and slowly crash-lands to the ground
Heartrending screams for home are the prevailing sounds
The chill takes a deep dive, freezing the marrow into my bones
Filling up my entire being with thoughts of escaping for home

The Lamentation of the Enslaved

Oh, Creator of all things, please, restore me to Africa I pray
Where the true sun's warmth as gifted to me every day
These chains are sapping my strength as they sickeningly sway
Painfully trapping my body -- but my mind will never be caged!
If that strange sun rises again tomorrow and still feels all wrong, we must recover our energy any way we can to come back strong

***

Caught!

Punishment for the enslaved who were caught while trying to escape could be horrendous. Starting with a very vicious and public beating and including limb amputation and branding for those who tried to escape multiple times.

The dogs bite my heels
I feel their hot breath and
Snapping jaws
Threatening to drag be back
Into the lion's maw
Closer and closer
They come
Until

"Well, lookee' here,
We done caught ourselves a
Ni**er!"

The Lamentation of the Enslaved

Bitten, beaten,

Dragged back to hell

My belly feels the roughness of the tree

Rope bites into my wrists

The whip

Tastes my blood and flesh

A scream loudly pierces my ear

Oh!

That was me.

***

The Golden Magnolia

Not all plantation homes were equal[xxiv]; some were essentially practical working houses. However, many were exorbitant and ornate. The Golden Magnolia was one such plantation home. The gravel road kicks up dirt as the wagons pull up to the house. Not everything is perfect and as the enslaved disembark, they look around questioningly, not knowing what lies before them.

All around they see others, working in the fields. The sun at Golden Magnolia always beats down with a vengeance. The enslaved are pushed hard to ensure that work is done on time and are severely punished if they are seen as lazy.

But how can anyone possibly not see that Golden Magnolia is a beautiful place! To have this 'home' they should feel so grateful and lucky.

The Lamentation of the Enslaved

The Golden Magnolia
Sounds like a beautiful flower
Yet for those who are slaves
On this land they do cower

The enslavers live in a large house
On the grounds with stately trees
But to the slaves in a shack
They pray upon on their knees

They sleep on straw
With dirt beneath their feet
They don't smell any flowers
In their mind they feel defeat

To Martha and to Samuel
Everything is fair
They give them a roof and food to eat
But to them, it is a nightmare

***

The Wisdom of Samuel Alford III - Colossians 3.22

While Mufa thinks about the internal tension that Samuel Alford III experiences with being an enslaver and a good Christian man, Samuel himself uses these words to help him overcome that tension.

Hate	What do you know of hate?
Does a dog hate	His master's discipline?
Or a mule hate	The strike of the whip?
Can a cow	Understand the cowbell?
Or a horse	Understand the bit?
Don't pretend	You're anything like me

You don't even understand what I say

A heritage rooted	In savagery
You're an ape,	Who was born to obey
Just because you	Resemble a man
Doesn't in any way	Make you human
Be thankful to me	For your rescue
From the barbarity	Of the place, you came from
I am like	Your personal saviour

The Lamentation of the Enslaved

For bringing you here to my home

The Bible says	In Colossians 3.22
Servants	Obey your masters
Even when	Your masters don't see you

***

Dear Massa

The word massa in this poem is a corruption of the word master which was a term used by the enslaved to refer to their enslavers as they were not permitted to use personal names.

Mufa is a thinking person. As a child of Nri, he was taught to think first and then act. He is the kind of enslaved person that many plantation owners secretly fear and hate. He learns to hide this trait for his safety. As life goes on at the Golden Magnolia, Mufa comes to realize the internal tension that Samuel Alford III often struggles with.

The Lamentation of the Enslaved

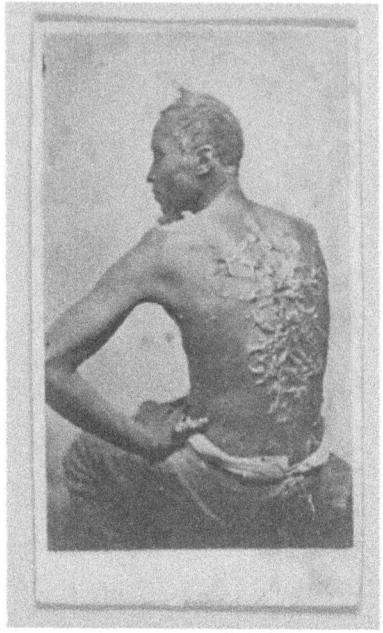

Figure 6 - Gordon Medical Exam - Collection of the Smithsonian National Museum of African American History and Culture 1863; printed later

Massa my heart breaks for you
For you are a dichotomy split in two

One part is what you could be
Your potential, your best possibility

Then there's the thing you always will be
Evil's personified in all its glory

For what is White but purity
A colour of virtuous epitome

Pure, pristine, unspoiled
God's colour one might think aloud
A beauteous thing unsoiled

> *My Black skin is a reminder*
> *Of sitting fearfully in the dark*
> *The home of pure malevolence*
> *And empty of benevolence*
> *An archetype of evil, colour of the corrupt*
> *It is my reality to drink of this immoral cup*

Dear Massa, I often wonder
How conflicted you must be
Purity of White on the outside
Covering your bestiality

Depravity burns within your heart
I feel it through your whip

Good and bad unreconciled
Putrefies your workmanship

The Lamentation of the Enslaved

Your time in the confessional
Hours spent on your knees

Praying to a deity
Following religious decrees

Dark is still your heart of hearts
While you beat on my black skin

Exchanging me for the demon that
Possesses you from within

> *I promise you that my black skin*
> *Shall forever be your weakness*
> *You will hate it with a passion*
> *While secretly admiring it for its sleekness*
> *My black life is a consequence of*
> *Your life of opulence*

Massa your proclivity to racism
Is as perverted as it is gruesome

Beating me so I cannot stand
Making me thank you and kiss your hand

While you sleep on your

Bed of feathers
I must rest on the cold hard ground

You enjoy all of your life's pleasure
But for me there no such thing as leisure

> *I make a vow, I will survive*
> *Beat me, starve me, work me to death*
> *I swear my children will contrive*
> *To find a way to live and thrive*
> *Yet right now you might murder me*
> *But my family will one day be free*

***

Mufa's Last Thoughts

The circle of life has brought our dear Mufa to death's door. As he lay in his bed of straw that fateful night, he thinks about his life.

I am a child of the Kingdom of Nri
My precious home that I will now never see
Oh, how I long for my beautiful homeland
For the long forgotten touch of my mother's hand
Is she alive, was she captured and enslaved
I sit with my head in my hands ashamed
I could not care for her as she got old
All of those choices taken out of my control
Now as I lay dying on this cold hard earth
My heart longs for the country of my birth
Now with my last breath remember me,

I am a child of the kingdom of Nri!
We believe all men are born to be free.
This gift is granted by Chukwu to all
that enter into Nri's great hall."

***

Mufa's Journey – A Retelling

Young
But a man
Suddenly captured by men stronger than him
Taken to the ocean where he is thrown on a boat

He is thrust into a large room at the bottom of the boat
That is full of men, women, and children

The boat started to move, and everyone was flung about
Mufa started feeling hot... light headed... like he is suffocating
The room started to spin... he can't breathe...
So many people
Crying. Screaming. Yelling. Wanting to be free

He was alone in a room full of people
Afraid … feeling sick to his stomach
What is happening to him?
How would his family find him when they didn't know he had been taken?
Where is he going?

White men came down with chains and ropes

The Lamentation of the Enslaved

Some of the men charged at them
They were immediately thrown to the ground
They were chained or tied with strong, thick ropes to the side of the boat
They threatened anyone who made any noise
That they would be next!

He was quiet so the White men let him be
He sees young children crying …abandoned
Where were their parents?
Although he is only 16, he goes to them to offer comfort
He has younger siblings and doesn't want them to feel so alone
He feels they need someone to be strong. To look out for them
He misses his mother and her love and feels …so alone

And then… as suddenly as the boat started
The boat stops…And everything is still

Everyone is herded like cattle
To waiting wagons
He is separated from the children
Who reach for him as they are dragged away crying
Dust covers his hair
Fills his nose and his mouth

As they travel down a long and empty road
They arrive at a town and are put on a platform
Where they are sold like grain
He is confused ...what is happening?

Finally, he and 3 others
1 man, 1 woman, and 1 young girl
Are put on another wagon
And taken to a large area of land with a
Large White house that looks inviting
...but looks are deceiving

Mufa takes in his surroundings
And is hopeful
Maybe he was mistaken
Maybe things will be ok

But then he is thrown into a shack
Where they used to keep animals
Now he and the others are treated like animals

And he knows his life has now changed
Forever

***

Make sure to read,

Enslaved, Chronicle of Resistance Book II
Freedom Bells Are Ringing

And

Enslaved, Chronicle of Resistance Book III
Hidden in Plain Sight

And

Enslaved, Chronicle of Resistance Book IV
A Companion Reader

Appendix 1 – Flyer of an escaped enslaved

A broadside with printed black text on off-White paper.

Large, bold text at the top reads [$1000 / REWARD!] Followed by smaller text reading [RAN AWAY from the subscribers on the night of the 5th inst. a NEGRO MAN named / George, / aged 22 or 23 years, 5 feet 7 or 8 inches in height] and goes on to describe his appearance and possible clothing, which includes [a green frock cloth coat, with a black velvet collar, a low-crowned White silk hat]. The text then continues on to describe [one negro BOY, aged 25 or twenty-six years; named / Jefferson], as well as [One negro girl named ESTHER (nicknamed Puss,) aged 17 or 18, black, tall, slim and regularly proportioned, - diffident and serious, embarrassed hen addressed, and at the same time picks or plays with fingers.] who is the sister of George, and [a girl named AMANDA, aged 15 or 16, a dark copper coloured mulatto, thick and heavy set, 5 ft. 4 inches high, has a sullen and impudent look, a large head of hair, and a green dress.] The text goes on to give the terms of the reward, which promised $300 for either George or Jefferson and $200 for either Esther or Amanda. At bottom left is [Germantown, Mason Co. Ky. / 20th January 1840] and at bottom right are the names of the posters: [ANDERSON DONIPHAN / JOSEPH FRAZEE / JOHN D. MORFORD]. There is considerable loss at the bottom right corner of the page. Collection of the Smithsonian National Museum of African American History and Culture, Gift from the Liljenquist Family Collection January 20, 1840

Table of Figures

FIGURE 1 - THE LAMENTATION OF THE ENSLAVED 15
FIGURE 2 - SLAVE SHIP - [[FILE:HOS D326 DECKS OF A SLAVE SHIP.JPG | HOS D326 DECKS OF A SLAVE SHIP]] BLAKE, WILLIAM O, PUBLIC DOMAIN, VIA WIKIMEDIA COMMONS 20
FIGURE 3 - RUNAWAY SLAVE - COLLECTION OF THE SMITHSONIAN NATIONAL MUSEUM OF AFRICAN AMERICAN HISTORY AND CULTURE, GIFT FROM THE LILJENQUIST FAMILY COLLECTION JANUARY 20, 1840 47
FIGURE 4 - SELLING SLAVES - AMERICAN ANTI-SLAVERY ALMANAC, PUBLIC DOMAIN, VIA WIKIMEDIA COMMONS 50
FIGURE 5 - MY CHILD - AMERICAN ANTI-SLAVERY ALMANAC, PUBLIC DOMAIN, VIA WIKIMEDIA COMMONS 89
FIGURE 6 - GORDON MEDICAL EXAM - COLLECTION OF THE SMITHSONIAN NATIONAL MUSEUM OF AFRICAN AMERICAN HISTORY AND CULTURE 1863; PRINTED LATER 112

Biographies and Poems

Brian Sankarsingh

SANKARSINGH is a Trinidadian-born Canadian immigrant who has published several books of poetry on a wide range of social and historical themes including racism, colonialism and enslavement. These topics are intimately intertwined with Sankarsingh's professional work with the Alliance for Healthier Communities. Sankarsingh artfully blends prose and poetry into his storytelling creating an eclectic mix with both genres. This unique approach is sure to provide something for everyone.

His debut book, A Sliver of a Chance, received several 5-star reviews from The Prairies Book Review, BookView Review, Red Headed Book Lover, OnlineBookClub and Readers Favourite.

Register of poems

1. A History Lesson – The Beginning
2. Humanity's Mourning
3. Mufa
4. eguzogidela
5. I am John Brown
6. Mufa's Despair at sea
7. Mufa's Loss
8. John Brown
9. The Auction I
10. The Auction II
11. Broken not Crushed
12. A Song of Remembrance
13. I am the Golden Magnolia
14. The Wisdom of Samuel Alford III – Know your place
15. I am Tom
16. My name is Mufa
17. I am Samuel Alford III
18. Clemency
19. The Wisdom of Samuel Alford III – Colossians 3:22
20. Dear Massa

Janet L. Wheat-Kaytor

Janet L. Wheat-Kaytor started writing poetry as a teen. It was a medium of expression like none other. Although Wheat-Kaytor continued to write over the years, she always kept these poems to personal and apart. Brian Sankarsingh asked to see some of her poetry, and she shared some of them. This is a difficult thing to do as they represented a part of her deepest self.

After reading her poems, Sankarsingh asked her to be a contributor to this book. Wheat-Kaytor stills continues to write poetry, and hopefully one day will complete her own book.

Register of poems

1. Mufa's Identity
2. Samuel Alford III
3. A Changed Young Girl Part I
4. A Changed Young Girl Part II
5. Freedom
6. Hidden Love Part I
7. Hidden Love Part II
8. My Beloved
9. The Golden Magnolia
10. Mufa's Journey – A retelling

J. E. Rehel

Photo credit: Ani Castillo

Jason is a writer, editor and, since age 4, a voracious reader of anything and everything, from sacred texts to dictionaries and everything in between. Jason is also a white, cis gender, male-leaning individual whose ancestors took part in the colonization of lands Mi'kmaq territory over 12 generations. Jason holds a degree in English literature and art history from McGill (slave-owner[5]) University, and he then edited and wrote arts journalism before engaging in work as a community health advocate and communications professional. Poetry is a longstanding love of his, across many forms and centuries. Jason seeks peace and better futures for all through his words and actions, and he was and is still humbled to be part of the Enslaved project. He hopes to continue to share and deliver on its goals of increased and deepened understandings about oppression, its causes and effects, and how to disrupt it.

1. The Ocean's Breath in His Ear
2. Winter in His Heart

---

[5] https://www.mcgill.ca/about/history/who-was-james-mcgill

Loretta Laurie Fisher

Loretta is a passionate writer, human rights activist, and community engagement worker. She works on behalf of members of society who desperately need their voices heard. As a member of Toronto's Partnership & Accountability Circle she takes her role as a respected Elder seriously.

Loretta's reports, articles, and poetry are published in various anthologies such as "Brilliance Is the Clothing I Wear!" published by Dundurn Press. Her byline is in Spring Mag: https://springmag.ca/author/laurie-fisher.

Loretta believes we must unite as one human race and actively embrace the positive changes needed to heal ourselves and the planet.

Register of poems

1. I am Human
2. Stripped!
3. For the Sake of Africa
4. Tricked and Stolen
5. Feewar's Final Promise

Sherman K Francis

Sherman K Francis was born and raised in Trinidad and Tobago in a community that did not uplift or promote excellence. Though poor, in this community everyone found ways to create or manufacture their own happiness. One could find a rare gem like his mother, whose determination ensured her three children were educated and could choose to excel or settle for mediocrity. This Sherman understood was the key to an abundance of opportunities.

At a very early age he enjoyed performing and would often provide comedy relief for his mother and two siblings before they retired for the night. Later on, he participated in the arts and thus became acutely observant of his environment. This allowed him to mature much faster than his peers and was ahead of his years in thinking and planning. He is a very talented and thoughtful artist and portrays in his work his ability to captivate and intrigue.

He is also very religious and allows nothing to interfere in his relationship with his God. Though it may not be visible from his appearance, he is very approachable and delights in working with those who are less fortunate. He relishes an opportunity to encourage and guide a youthful mind to make constructive choices. He has developed several close

The Lamentation of the Enslaved

relationships with the elderly and some of the women have been adopted as his mothers.

He never envisioned himself being able to travel but has thus had the opportunity to visit several countries which has broadened his worldview. He now resides in a very remote part of the United States where he writes and practices as a Naturopathic Doctor and Natural Health Consultant.

Register of poems

1. The Land Speaks
2. A Helpless Cry
3. Conversation with Massa

Index

[i] Black and White: Why capitalization matters - https://www.cjr.org/analysis/language_corner_1.php
[ii] The First Africans in Virginia Landed in 1619. It Was a Turning Point for Slavery in American History—But Not the Beginning - https://time.com/5653369/august-1619-jamestown-history/
[iii] African Americans at Jamestown - https://www.nps.gov/jame/learn/historyculture/african-americans-at-jamestown.htm
[iv] Eli Whitney's Patent for the Cotton Gin - https://www.archives.gov/education/lessons/cotton-gin-patent
[v] Boddy-Evans, Alistair. "A Short History of the African Slave Trade." ThoughtCo, Aug. 26, 2020, thoughtco.com/african-slavery-101-44535 - https://www.thoughtco.com/african-slavery-101-44535
[vi] Is Africa the cradle of humanity? - https://science.howstuffworks.com/life/evolution/africa-cradle-humanity.htm
[vii] The Nri Kingdom (900AD – Present): Rule by theocracy - https://thinkafrica.net/nri-nigeria/
[viii] 7 Important Things to Know About Eze Nri - https://www.ndiigbofest.com/2020/07/29/7-important-things-to-know-about-eze-nri/
[ix] Igbo - https://omniglot.com/writing/igbo.htm
[x] Barracoon - https://en.wikipedia.org/wiki/Barracoon
[xi] Slave Ships and Maritime Archaeology: An Overview - https://www.jstor.org/stable/20853144
[xii] The Amistad - https://www.history.com/topics/slavery/amistad-case
[xiii] The Five Stages of Grief – An Examination of the Kubler-Ross Model - https://www.psycom.net/depression.central.grief.html
[xiv] The Tale of the Nri - https://www.nzukobrand.com/post/the-tale-of-nri
[xv] Slave Auction, 1859 - http://www.eyewitnesstohistory.com/slaveauction.htm
[xvi] Henry Bibb aka Henry Walton Bibb https://en.wikipedia.org/wiki/Henry_Bibb
[xvii] Understanding the long-run effects of Africa's slave trades - https://voxeu.org/article/understanding-long-run-effects-africa-s-slave-

trades

[xviii] The Impact of Slavery on Modern Africa - https://www.fairplanet.org/dossier/beyond-slavery/the-impact-of-slavery-on-modern-africa/

[xix] Death Toll From The Slave Trade The African Holocaust - http://www.worldfuturefund.org/Reports/Slavedeathtoll/slaverydeathtoll.html

[xx] American Slavery As It Is: Testimony of a Thousand Witnesses - https://archive.org/details/DKC0106

[xxi] Incidents in the Life of a Slave Girl, Written by Herself Linda Brent (Harriet Jacobs) - https://wps.ablongman.com/wps/media/objects/1510/1546451/pdfs/incidents.pdf

[xxii] Narrative of the Life and Adventures of Henry Bibb, an American Slave, Written by Himself - https://docsouth.unc.edu/neh/bibb/summary.html

[xxiii] Relationships Among Slaves: An Overview - https://www.encyclopedia.com/humanities/applied-and-social-sciences-magazines/relationships-among-slaves-overview

[xxiv] 21 Southern mansions & plantation homes from the Old South - https://clickamericana.com/topics/home-garden/stunning-southern-mansions-plantation-homes

www.ingramcontent.com/pod-product-compliance
Lightning Source LLC
Chambersburg PA
CBHW020934090426
42736CB00010B/1140